World Issues

THE ARMS TRADE

Clive Gifford

Chrysalis Education

WORLD ISSUES

ABORTION	EQUAL OPPORTUNITIES	HUMAN RIGHTS
ANIMAL RIGHTS	EUTHANASIA	POVERTY
ARMS TRADE	FOOD TECHNOLOGY	RACISM
CAPITAL PUNISHMENT	GENETIC ENGINEERING	REFUGEES
CONSUMERISM	GENOCIDE	TERRORISM
DRUGS		

Distributed in the United States by
Smart Apple Media
1980 Lookout Drive
North Mankato, Minnesota 56003

Copyright © Chrysalis Books Group Plc 2004

ISBN: 1-59389-154-7

Library of Congress Control Number: 2003116683

Produced by Tall Tree Ltd.

Editorial Manager: Joyce Bentley
Editor: Clare Lewis
Project Editor: Jon Richards
Designer: Ben Ruocco
Picture Researcher: Lorna Ainger
Educational Consultant: Lizzy Bacon
Americaniser: Margaret Parrish

Printed in Hong Kong.

Picture Acknowledgments
The Publishers would like to thank the following for their kind permission to reproduce
the photographs:
Aviation-Images.com/Pennings: 47
Corbis: Philip James Corwin 9c, Michael S. Lewis 8, Michael S. Yamashita 46, AFP 48
Digital Vision: 20, 21, 31, 35
Getty Images: AFP 48, Natalie Behring 9t, CNN 24, Stephen Chernin 14, Daily Mirror 39,
David Greedy 18, Chris Hondros 25, Robert Nickelsberg 45, Spencer Platt 29, Edy
Purnomo 36, Space Imaging 13, Mario Tama 12, 23, Ami Vitale 28
PA Photos: Ben Curtis 51, EPA 16, 27, 30, 33, 37, 40, 44, 50
Rex Features Ltd.: Ponopresse 49
Still Pictures: Sebastian Bolesch 19, 42, Mark Edwards 41, Ton Koene 9b
Topham: 10, AP 43
TRH Pictures: 11, 15, 17, 22, 26, 32, 34, 38

CONTENTS

Kendu's Story

Taken from his home at a young age, Kendu Mbosi has seen the damage that the arms trade has caused in just one country. In his time as a child soldier, he has come across a wide range of weapons designed and made in many countries around the world. These have caused devastation to his comrades, his friends, his home, and his family.

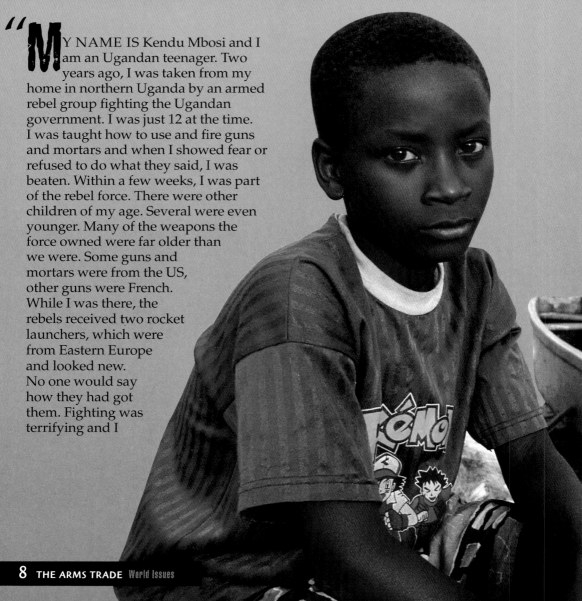

"MY NAME IS Kendu Mbosi and I am an Ugandan teenager. Two years ago, I was taken from my home in northern Uganda by an armed rebel group fighting the Ugandan government. I was just 12 at the time. I was taught how to use and fire guns and mortars and when I showed fear or refused to do what they said, I was beaten. Within a few weeks, I was part of the rebel force. There were other children of my age. Several were even younger. Many of the weapons the force owned were far older than we were. Some guns and mortars were from the US, other guns were French. While I was there, the rebels received two rocket launchers, which were from Eastern Europe and looked new. No one would say how they had got them. Fighting was terrifying and I saw many people die. I was lucky and managed to escape and be reunited with my family. The village we used to live in is no longer there—much of it was destroyed by bombs.

We all now live in a large town in southern Uganda. Life is hard, we miss our village, and I have to help care for my younger sister. She lost her left leg when her bicycle rode over a landmine buried near our village. I try to forget the bad memories of the fighting, but sometimes they return. I know that there would be troubles between different groups in Uganda even if there were no weapons, but I think the weapons make it much harder, especially on ordinary people. I was lucky. My mother, my sister, and I are still alive."

The Impact of Arms Trading

The dangers of arms trading impact all parts of the world, both human and natural.

AFGHANISTAN
In Afghanistan, an estimated four million landmines lie hidden as a result of over 20 years of bitter conflict. In 2000, some 2,400 Afghans were victims of landmines.

UNITED STATES
On an average day in the United States, around ten children and youths under the age of 20 die from gun-related violence. This means that more children and teenagers in the US die from firearms than from cancer, pneumonia, influenza, asthma, and HIV/AIDS combined.

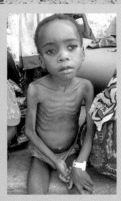

ERITREA
Billions are spent on arms by countries whose people are poor. The war-torn African nation of Eritrea spends more than a quarter of all of its income on its military forces, while its people are among the poorest in the world.

What Is The Arms Trade?

The arms industry is engaged in researching, designing, and building military technology, particularly weapons and protection against weapons, such as armor. The arms trade is the buying and selling of arms. It is a vast industry, one of the largest in the world, and it has major effects on how millions of people live their lives.

Sir Basil Zaharof (1850–1936) was knighted by King George V of the UK and decorated by the French government for his services in supplying arms to the Allies during World War I.

THE ARMS TRADE is not a new or 20th-century phenomenon. It can be traced back hundreds of years to the invention of new weapons and their demand by different groups, forces, and countries. The arrival of gunpowder in Europe from the late 14th century onward led to a demand by various armies for gunpowder-charged muskets and cannons.

During the 18th and 19th centuries, the Industrial Revolution and the rise of large factories saw companies able to build large numbers of more complicated weapons, such as machine guns and massive warships. These arms were touted for sale by powerful weapons traders, such as Sir Basil Zaharof (see left). These businessmen did not care who bought their weapons and they sold arms to all sides engaged in a conflict.

How has the arms trade developed?

The two world wars of the 20th century both saw massive jumps in weapons technology, the range of weapons available, and the numbers built and sold. For example, at the start of World War I (1914–1918) aircraft were flimsy and unreliable machines. They were used only in very small numbers and in a limited role as reconnaissance aircraft

An image from a Boeing factory during World War II showing row upon row of B-17 Flying Fortress bombers being built.

or "spotters," reporting the positions of troops and guns on the ground. By the end of the war, however, they had been developed into a range of different types, including bombers and fighters, that were able to fly higher, farther, and faster than any aircraft at the start of the conflict. The first tanks were also introduced in World War I, and although these machines were slow and cumbersome at first, they went on to change the tactics and structure of modern warfare. Both tanks and aircraft developed greatly and were built in huge numbers in the period between the two wars to arm the forces that later fought in World War II (1939–1945). Enormous arms companies, such as Boeing and Lockheed in the US, were established and grew to supply these new, sophisticated weapons in ever increasing numbers.

What was the Cold War and how did it affect the arms trade?

From the end of World War II until the early 1990s, many countries of the world aligned themselves with one of the two superpowers, the US or the Soviet Union. The world's two most powerful nations were hostile to and suspicious of each other but never directly fought. This period is known as the Cold War and it saw an expansion of the arms industry and the development of giant arms and aerospace companies. In the late 1970s and early 1980s, more arms were bought and sold than at any other time in history.

These soldiers are training at Fort Benning, Georgia. This army base has, in the past, trained some of the people the US has fought against in Central and South America.

The two superpowers built up larger and larger stockpiles of weapons within their own borders, while spending vast sums on research into new types of arms, including nuclear weapons. In addition, the superpowers and their major allies supplied many other nations and forces with large amounts of arms. Sometimes, these arms were donated or offered at greatly reduced prices to governments in order to build alliances with other countries against the other superpower. Some of these weapons supplies were donated to rebel groups in countries whose governments were friendly to the other superpower. The goal was to topple these governments and replace them with others that were more friendly.

What has happened since the Cold War?

With the collapse of the Soviet Union at the start of the 1990s, there were no longer two rival superpowers. The threat

of all-out war between the world's most powerful nations receded and the US, Russia, and many of their major allies scaled down the size of their military forces. This resulted in a large surplus of arms, many of which were sold abroad. New military spending decreased a great deal, but not at a rate that many peace campaigners had hoped for. The remaining superpower, the US, still spends more on the military every year than the next 20 largest spenders combined. Arms companies started to look for new markets in other parts of the world where there were conflicts or tensions, such as in the Middle East as well as in many parts of Africa and Asia. For example, Pakistan and India, engaged in a long-running dispute over the region of Kashmir, bought over $18 billion worth of weapons during the 1990s.

As a symbol of the amount of money the US spends on weapons, the Pentagon, just outside Washington, D.C., serves as the headquarters of the world's biggest military force.

Racing on their own

"For 45 years of the Cold War we were in an arms race with the Soviet Union. Now it appears we're in an arms race with ourselves."

Admiral Eugene Carroll Jr., US Navy (ret),
Deputy Director, Center for Defense Information

How much is the arms trade worth today?

According to the Stockholm International Peace Research Institute, the total amount of money spent on the world's military forces in 2001 was $839 billion—that is over $130 for every single man, woman, and child on the planet. Five countries account for over half of all military expenditure, while the 15 biggest spenders together spend over three-quarters. A large part of this enormous sum goes on paying, housing, and looking after the millions of people who are members of military forces. Yet, at least $50 billion is spent on arms worldwide every year. To put that sum into perspective, the arms trade every year is worth more than 20 times the size of the entire annual budget for the United Nations.

The United Nations Security Council meets to determine any threats to peace or acts of aggression and to suggest a course of action.

Who are the biggest sellers?

Although over 100 nations of the world build and sell arms, the vast majority of weapons sales is concentrated in the hands of a small number of nations. Some 85 percent of the money spent on arms by countries and groups throughout the world goes to companies and organizations that are based in just five countries; the US, the UK, Russia, France, and China. These five countries also happen to be some of the permanent members of the United Nations Security Council, the part of the United Nations that decides on how to maintain peace and security throughout the world.

Is the arms trade legal?

Much of the arms trade is legal and part of the world economy and general global trade in goods and services that flows from one country to another. However, there is also a large forbidden or illegal arms trade, especially in smaller, easier-to-transport weapons. Illegal arms trading can involve selling stolen or illegally obtained weapons. It can also involve selling weapons and equipment to outlawed groups and guerrilla fighters or to countries that are prohibited from receiving weapons, sometimes by an international agreement such as a United Nations embargo on arms sales (see page 46).

A number of Tornado jets were sold by the UK to Saudi Arabia as part of the Al Yamamah arms deal, the biggest single arms deal to date.

What Is Bought And Sold In The Arms Trade?

Arms manufacturers sell a huge and bewildering array of items, from the simplest policeman's nightstick and the smallest bullet, to complex electronic navigation systems and the largest aircraft carrier.

Countries and organizations wishing to buy weapons can view them and deal with suppliers at arms fairs that are held all over the world.

A TYPICAL MAJOR ARMS fair will have dozens of stands selling thousands of different products. Most of the arms on sale are conventional weapons—those arms which are not chemical, biological, or nuclear weapons (see pages 20–21). Major conventional weapons are aircraft, submarines, warships such as destroyers and aircraft carriers, tanks and armored vehicles, as well as large artillery guns and missile systems.

These weapons form the most expensive and profitable side of the arms trade, accounting for as much as 80 percent of the value of all arms sales. New conventional weapons tend to be incredibly expensive. A Mirage Rafale jet fighter, for example, costs around $60 million and can carry a range of missiles, many of which cost several hundred thousand dollars each. One missile, called Storm Shadow, is believed to cost nearly $2 million per unit.

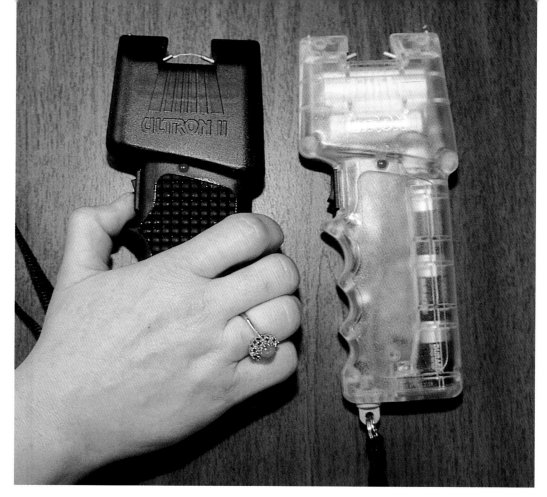

These tazer guns are designed to shoot a charge of electricity through a person to immobilize them without killing them.

Does the arm trade sell weapons only to the military?

Far from it. Police forces, prisons, and other security organizations in many countries around the world buy arms, such as handguns and assault rifles, as well as a range of products designed to restrain prisoners and to control crowds. These include armored vehicles, water cannons, gas sprays, riot shields, and electro-shock devices, such as tazer guns. Many of these items have caused concern among human rights groups, since they have been used for torture and beatings. Although weaponry is an important part of many arms sales, vast sums are also spent on materials and services that are related to these weapons, such as maintenance and training contracts, as well as transportation equipment. For example, by 2010, the British Royal Air Force (RAF) is expected to have spent as much as $36 million on the HST. This is an advanced flight simulator used to train pilots to fly the Hawk jet aircraft. As military weapons have become more and more complex, services such as training have become an important commodity. They are promoted and sold at arms fairs and meetings almost as much as bullets, bombs, and other weapons.

Small arms, big headache

"Small arms are easy to buy: in some places, an AK–47 assault rifle can be bought for as little as $15, or even for a bag of grain. They are easy to use: with minimal training, even a child can wield one... Most of all, they are deadly."

Kofi Annan, UN Secretary General, 2001

What is the small arms trade?

Small arms are usually defined as weapons for personal use, such as handguns, rifles, and light machine guns, and weapons that can be operated by a single person, such as grenades, mortars, and antipersonnel landmines.

The building and selling of large conventional weapons such as jet aircraft is concentrated in a handful of wealthier countries. In contrast, small arms are manufactured legally in more than 600 factories in over 95 countries throughout the world. Out of these countries, at least 50 less developed countries are producing small arms, and 26 are selling them abroad. The legal trade in small arms was estimated in 2000 to be worth between $5 billion and $6 billion. The illegal trade in small arms, which are easy to hide and transport, is feared to be even larger.

Nearly all of the 70 million Russian–style AK–47s produced in the past are still in operation. AK–47s can fire around 600 rounds in a minute.

How many small arms are around?

The United Nations estimates that over 500 million small arms are found around the world—one for every 12 people. During the Cold War, many nations were flooded with small arms by powerful nations such as the United States and the former Soviet Union and their allies. These arms remain in countries, while stockpiles of old weapons from previous conflicts are traded and used in other conflicts. Many small arms are easy to maintain and last for decades, such as the Russian-designed AK-47 assault rifle. These weapons are often cheap enough for there to be plenty of buyers, including criminals and rebel militia groups.

DEBATE—Are small arms the problem?

- Yes. Small arms may not start conflicts but they often cause them to escalate quickly. The low cost and ready availability of small arms often tempts people to solve problems using violence rather than debate. The vast majority of modern conflicts are fought with small arms, which kill over 1,000 people a day.

- No. Small arms are not illegal for adults to own in many countries. They do not start conflicts themselves—disagreements between different peoples or groups are usually the cause.

Many weapons, including the AK-47, are easy to use and maintain. As such, they remain a popular choice of weapon for many forces, including those that train and use children as soldiers.

What are weapons of mass destruction?

Weapons of mass destruction (WMDs) are weapons designed to kill large numbers of people. WMDs include nuclear weapons, chemical weapons, and biological weapons.

When were WMDs first used?

Biological or germ warfare involves using parts or products of living things to cause harm. By trying to poison the drinking wells of a castle or throwing the bodies of plague victims into an opposing army, armed forces have used forms of biological warfare since medieval times. The first major use of chemical warfare was during World War I, when chlorine gas, mustard gas, and phosgene gas were first deployed by German forces against the Allies. Although there have been hundreds of tests of nuclear weapons, only two have ever been used in war—the two atomic bombs dropped on the Japanese cities of Hiroshima and Nagasaki by the United States at the end of World War II in 1945.

A mushroom cloud caused by a nuclear explosion. The nuclear weapons that are kept by armed forces today are many times more powerful than the bombs dropped on Hiroshima and Nagasaki.

These US troops are wearing special suits to protect them from nuclear, chemical, and biological attacks. The production of these suits is another aspect of the arms trade.

Why are WMDs used so rarely?

The military forces of almost all countries have studied the effects of WMDs and realize that they have limited military usefulness. Their effects are hard to control, many contaminate areas for decades afterward, and their use on another country is likely to trigger an extreme response in reply. International agreements, such as the Nuclear Non-Proliferation Treaty (1968) and the 1925 Geneva Protocol, have also sought to outlaw the spread and use of weapons of mass destruction. However, fears remain about these devastating weapons. Chemical weapons, for example, were used in the 1980s during both the Iran-Iraq war and by Iraqi forces on the Kurdish civilian population.

How many nations have WMDs?

At least 20 nations are known to have had programs producing chemical and biological weapons. There are seven nations with declared nuclear weapons; the US, Russia, the UK, France, China, India, and Pakistan. Israel is thought to have nuclear capability as well, while a few other nations, including North Korea, are believed to be developing nuclear weapons. A key concern is that the technology required to make these weapons could fall into the hands of terrorist groups that might actually use them. Many of the substances or equipment needed to make WMDs are easily available or are dual-use products, meaning that they have a peacetime use as well as a military one.

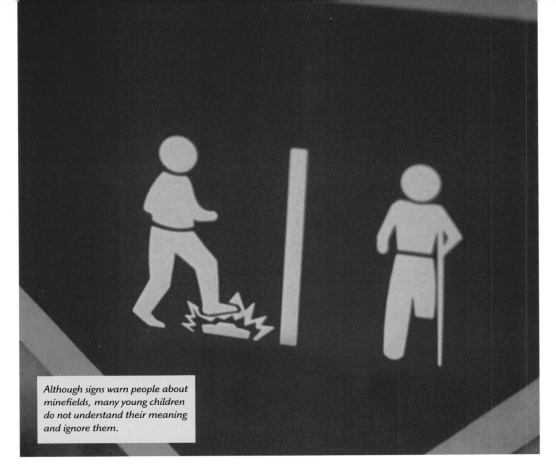

Although signs warn people about minefields, many young children do not understand their meaning and ignore them.

What are the particular problems with landmines?

Antipersonnel landmines are hidden killers. Buried just below the land's surface, they are hard to detect. They explode when pressure is placed on them from above, not knowing whether their victim is a soldier or civilian, an adult or a child. Landmines are one of the few weapons to remain dangerous long after the war or conflict which saw them laid has finished. Deaths attributed to 40-year-old landmines have been reported. Many minefields remain unknown; they were created without warning signs and barriers or these have since disappeared. In addition, some mines have been moved to new areas by floods or subsidence. The impact of landmines around the world is huge.

Poor farming communities have been particularly hard hit. Thousands of acres of land, often good farmland, have had to be left abandoned because of landmines planted there.

How common are landmines and landmine victims?

Surveys estimate that there are at least 50 million landmines buried throughout the world. On average, someone is killed or injured by a landmine every 15 minutes. The vast majority of landmine victims are civilians, mostly children. An estimated 300,000 children have been left severely disabled by landmines, which cause horrific injuries and often loss of limbs. This situation has led to a partially successful campaign to stop antipersonnel landmines from being used.

Can landmines be removed?

Yes. New technologies—in the form of special radar systems and mine clearing robots—are being developed, but the majority of mine location and removal is done by hand. Mine clearing personnel use a range of tools, including metal detectors and metal prodders, to probe the ground. Sometimes dogs are used to locate the scent of the mine's explosive. Clearing a mined area, though, is a slow, expensive, and risky business. It takes approximately 100 times longer to clear an area of mines than to sow it with mines in the first place.

The costs of landmines

Some 54 countries have produced more than 340 models of antipersonnel landmines. They cost as little as $3 to produce and are relatively easy to deploy. By contrast, it costs between $300 and $1,000 to locate and destroy a single mine.

Source: Adopt-A-Minefield Campaign

These hospital patients show the terrible extent of the injuries suffered by landmine victims.

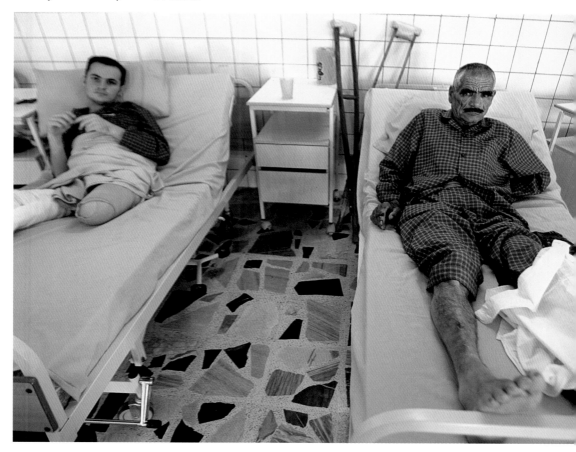

Who Buys And Sells Arms?

An arms sale or transaction is usually shown publicly as a deal negotiated between two governments or between a government and a company. In reality, the buying and selling of arms can be far more complicated.

MOST OF THE world's arms are bought by governments who are known as state actors. Nonstate actors who also buy arms, often illegally, are usually rebels or groups that seek to topple the government of a country. Among the state actors, the United States government remains the single biggest customer for arms, nearly all of which are bought from companies based on its own soil. The biggest buyers of arms from other countries tend to be Asian and Middle Eastern nations such as Saudi Arabia, China, India, Pakistan, South Korea, and Taiwan, although almost all nations enter the arms market to buy conventional weapons and small arms from other countries at some point.

Victor Bout is a Russian arms trader who has sold weapons to a number of regimes and rebels in Africa and Asia.

Many weapons have found their way to conflicts in the African nations of Sierra Leone and Liberia, despite embargoes imposed by the UN.

Who sells arms?

The defense departments of many countries, as well as private and state-owned companies, sell arms to both state and nonstate actors. In the majority of cases, arms companies follow the laws or rulings made by their government as well as any international agreements. In the UK, for example, the majority of arms sales to foreign nations or organizations have to gain approval from the government. Once these sales have been justified, the companies are then awarded an export license to allow the deal to take place. Since the end of the Cold War, however, the global arms market has become a lot smaller and, as a result, the competition to sell weapons has become far more intense. This can lead to organizations and individuals using bribes and other illegal tactics in order to complete a deal. It can also result in buyers and sellers using "middle men" to arrange a deal on their behalf and to disguise the sale of arms to countries or groups that have been forbidden from buying weapons by national or international agreements.

This submachine gun was manufactured by Heckler and Koch. The company has also brokered legal arms deals with armed forces all around the world.

What is brokering?

Brokering usually means buying arms in one foreign country, transporting them and then selling them in another foreign country. All of these deals and movements occur frequently without the weapons ever reaching the home country of the broker. In the UK, companies and individuals who engage in brokering do not have to apply for export licenses from the government or gain any other type of official approval. Sometimes, brokering is engaged in secretly, and in some cases a country sells arms to one nation, only to find out that some or all of these arms are then sold on to another nation, which the original country had no intention of selling to.

An arms trader talks

"I would say that the arms trade is now more powerful than during the years of the Cold War... every country is trying to sell as much as they can without restrictions... All governments are hypocritical about the arms trade. They keep business out of the public eye whilst selling as much as they possibly can... Also many buyers want to keep their purchases secret and suppliers have to agree or they may lose their contracts... Nowadays a middle-man like me can expect to make between a half- and two-percent commission on a deal... but you can make big money if you are prepared to deal with embargoed countries. In one deal for artillery shells with Libya the available commission was 35 percent."

Source: *New Internationalist* magazine, issue 261

What is the boomerang effect?

Weapons sold by one country are often eventually used in action against their own military forces. This is known as the boomerang effect, and it is not a new phenomenon. During World War I, German forces found both Belgian troops to the west and Russian troops to the east equipped with the same weapons as themselves. Many examples of the boomerang effect still occur today. For example, US-made weapons have been turned against US troops in Somalia, Iraq, Panama, and Haiti. In some cases, governments that were allies of the US were replaced.

The new leaders then turned out to be hostile to the US and inherited US-made weapons. For example, the US supplied arms to Afghan forces to help in their fight against the invading Soviet army in the 1980s, only to find these weapons turned against them when US-led forces invaded the country to topple the Taliban regime 20 years later in 2002. The same happened with Iraqi forces, who were armed by many Western companies during the country's war against Iran during the 1980s. Many of these weapons were then used against Western forces in the Gulf Wars of 1991 and 2003.

Many brokered deals take place at arms fairs, where organizations and representatives from a country can meet without setting foot on the home soil of either party.

Are There Benefits From The Arms Trade?

The arms trade makes up one percent of the entire world's trade. Billions of dollars change hands between buyers and sellers. Such an enormous industry, one of the world's largest, could not continue if both buyers and sellers did not believe there were benefits. The debate is over whether these benefits are genuine or important enough to justify such great expense.

These troops are involved in the struggle over the region of Jammu and Kashmir, an area whose territory is disputed by the nations of India and Pakistan.

EVERY INDIVIDUAL, GROUP, and nation strives to feel secure and safe. The governments of countries have a duty to protect their population and the territory which they inhabit. For centuries, this has been a key reason for nations building strong military forces and equipping them with effective weapons.

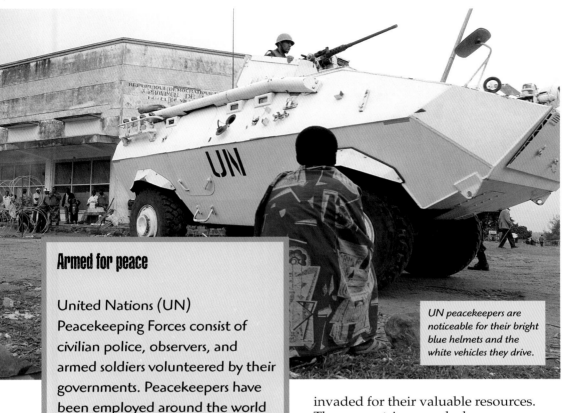

UN peacekeepers are noticeable for their bright blue helmets and the white vehicles they drive.

Armed for peace

United Nations (UN) Peacekeeping Forces consist of civilian police, observers, and armed soldiers volunteered by their governments. Peacekeepers have been employed around the world to restore or maintain peace, to help disarm former fighters, and to help areas rebuild. In 2001, 47,800 UN Peacekeepers were on duty. The arms carried by peacekeepers are considered vital for them to perform their important role.

It is the most frequently given reason for buying arms today and is backed by international laws and treaties that give nations the right to defend their borders. Some countries have developed valuable industries or have discovered extremely profitable deposits of raw materials, in particular fossil fuels such as oil. Many countries in this situation, such as the oil-producing nations of the Middle East, fear that they may be invaded for their valuable resources. These countries spend a large proportion of the wealth generated by these precious resources on arms to protect them.

Where are arms actually used?

Most of the arms actually used in anger today are not used directly to defend a country's borders or resources from attack by another country. Many nations have used their arms to invade other countries. Many more have used their weapons on their own people, either to suppress local opposition to their government or to fight bitter and long-running wars with rebel groups. A development report from the United Nations, which counted 82 armed conflicts in the world between 1989 and 1999, noted that 79 of these conflicts took place within the borders of a single country and involved civil wars or armed uprisings.

North Korea spends a large percentage of its national budget on weapons and the armed forces. It uses state occasions to parade its military strength.

What is a deterrent?

Arms may be bought but not used in the hope that a country's military strength will make another country decide against attacking or invading. This is known as a deterrent, and the most well-known example occurred during the Cold War with nuclear weapons. The US and the Soviet Union stockpiled vast numbers of nuclear warheads so that even a massive attack by one nation would leave the other with enough capability to launch an equally huge attack on the other. Some argue that this example is proof of how arms can be a deterrent. Others point to how a build-up of non-nuclear arms has not acted as a deterrent in many of the conflicts currently occurring around the world.

What is prestige purchasing?

The governments of many countries view their armed forces as an important symbol of their independence and power. The leaders of some nations buy large weapons, such as aircraft carriers or the latest jet fighters, in the belief that owning such weapons will make their country appear more important. They may also see a link between military might and political power, and will spend huge sums of money to expand

An intercontinental ballistic missile blasts clear of its silo. During the Cold War, both the US and the Soviet Union stockpiled hundreds of intercontinental ballistic missiles (ICBMs), which are capable of hitting a target thousands of miles away.

DEBATE—Do arms act as a deterrent, preventing conflict?

- Yes. Statistics show that most weapons purchased are never used. They are necessary for security and a deterrent.
- No. The deterrent effect of arms is overrated and leads to a massive waste of funds. The threat of attack or war has not stopped many countries from entering into conflicts with others.

their armed forces. They then openly display these forces in shows of strength meant to impress and intimidate their own people and other countries around the world. This is known as prestige purchasing. It is often extremely wasteful, since the weapons bought may not be suited to the region in which they are to operate. An example of this is Thailand's proposed buying of two Israeli submarines. Much of the local waters around Thailand are very shallow, making submarines an easy target. The sudden and cheap availability of some weapons also leads to prestige purchasing. For example, the end of the Cold War led to stocks of weapons flooding the market at low prices. Some countries bought weapons they could not afford before at what they saw as a bargain price.

Why do countries sell arms?

Countries sell arms or allow companies based in their country to sell arms for many reasons. Some of the most important reasons are about economics. The arms trade is split geographically with the majority of the manufacturers and sellers of arms based in the wealthier, more developed nations of the world. The arms trade in these countries is seen as a major employer of workers and the most, or one of the most, important industries for selling products abroad and bringing money into the country. Having a powerful and advanced arms industry is also a source of prestige for some nations. Arms companies often have a great deal of influence on governments. As a result, many critics feel that the economic importance of the arms trade to a country is exaggerated.

How do governments help arms companies?

Developing and testing new weapons is a phenomenally expensive business. Companies often need to sell not only to their own country's military but also to the military forces of other nations in order to make a profit. The US

Many workers in richer countries are dependant on jobs in the weapons industry.

The British royal family, including Prince Andrew (right), has been actively involved in promoting UK weapons companies to foreign nations.

government, for example, assists its country's arms companies by spending billions of dollars on research and development contracts. It also helps by actively promoting arms sales to other nations. Governments often support their nation's arms trade by sending ministers and officials to other nations to discuss deals. In the UK, for example, a government agency, funded by the taxpayer and employing 600 staff, called the Defence Export Services Organisation is devoted to helping arms companies sell abroad. Governments also provide low-cost or interest-free loans, offer insurance against another country failing to pay, and many other subsidies besides. The Campaign Against Arms Trade (CAAT) estimates that the UK arms export industry receives a government subsidy of around $1.2 billion every year.

The UK arms trade in numbers

The UK is the world's second-largest arms supplier behind the US and has a 20–25 percent share of the entire world market in legal sales. The UK's arms trade accounts for two percent of the country's exports, a third of the value of its exports of motor vehicles. Government figures indicate that it employs around 70,000 people, less than 0.3 percent of the entire workforce.

Sources: CAAT, the Oxford Group and Oxfam, UK

Has arms research led to useful civilian products?

Yes, research and development for military ends has led to the creation many products with important benefits for peaceful society. Radar, for example, which enables airliners to navigate safely, was developed as a military early warning system and used in World War II, while the military computer network called ARPAnet was the forerunner of the Internet. Critics argue that these and other advances may have been possible, and at a far lower cost, by investing in civil scientific research rather than in military development.

What other reasons are given for countries selling arms?

Countries and companies that sell arms use a number of arguments to justify their sales other than money. One of the most important is that selling arms can increase a country's influence in a part of the world. Arms sales have been used to bring two nations closer together to form an alliance, as happened during the Cold War when weapons were sold to countries allied to the US and the Soviet Union. Arms sales are often part of a package of other deals for sharing information or resources or supplying nonmilitary goods and services.

Without radar, air traffic control would be impossible and the amount of international civilian flights would be greatly reduced.

The F-16 is one of the most widely sold fighter jets in the world. Countries including Israel and the United Arab Emirates have bought these aircraft from the US.

DEBATE – Should government money be used to assist the arms trade?

- Yes. Government money helps the arms trade to employ over 500 000 people worldwide. All these jobs would be threatened if funding was withdrawn.
- No. Most of the people working in the arms trade are highly skilled and could easily find other work. If the government money was spent instead on essential services such as health and education, many more people would benefit.

Arms sales can be used to help control other countries, as the buyers become reliant on supplies of arms and expertise from the selling country. Weapons tend to be made up of hundreds and thousands of delicate and complex parts. Losing access to spare parts or further sales can help force countries into remaining friendly. Countries that sell arms develop high levels of knowledge about their customers' military strengths. Not only do they know the abilities of the weapons they sell, but they also tend to learn much about a nation's other weapons and the size of their forces. This, it is argued, can become vital should both nations come to conflict.

What is strategic balance?

Strategic balance is the idea that by selling the right amount of arms to different countries it is possible to build a balance of military power in a region. Each country's weapons act as a deterrent to the others and the balance keeps the peace. Critics argue that trying to achieve a balance of power in a region is difficult or impossible when there are several countries that can supply arms. If anything, it often results in an arms race (see page 37). It is simply not possible to create strategic balance when countries are of dramatically different sizes, populations, and wealth. For instance, the tiny nation of Singapore could not defend itself should China decide to invade, no matter how many conventional weapons it owned.

What Problems Does The Arms Trade Cause?

For some people, the arms trade is simply a business selling products and it cannot be held responsible for how they are used. However, many critics of the arms trade believe that selling large amounts of arms around the world helps to create conflicts, helps small-scale conflicts mushroom into larger scale wars, and causes physical and economic misery for millions of people.

WITHOUT ARMS supplies, wars are still possible, but many people believe they would be easier to contain, create fewer casualties, and be easier to end and rebuild in peace afterward. The relatively ready availability of arms can also prompt peoples or governments to seek a violent solution to a problem when peaceful solutions are available. Arms are also frequently used on a country's own people, who may not have taken up

Tear gas is used by police to disperse a peaceful demonstration in Indonesia.

These Tamil Tiger fighters are part of a guerrilla force that is fighting for an independent state in northern Sri Lanka.

arms but simply disagreed with their government's policies. The use of arms on peaceful demonstrators, critics, and protesters has, in countries from Indonesia and Sri Lanka to Uganda, Colombia, and Angola, caused troubles to escalate into violent conflict.

What is an arms race?

An arms race is a continuing cycle of rival nations feeling threatened by one another and buying or producing more and more weapons. The Cold War saw a massive arms race between the two rival superpowers, the US and the Soviet Union. Today, arms races are occurring in several regions around the world, such as between China and Taiwan and between India and Pakistan. Internal arms races can also occur within a country when a rebel group's purchase of weapons prompts the national government to spend more on arms. These arms races can create extra tension and instability, which can spill over into conflict. Even if an uneasy peace is kept, the money spent on weapons may escalate, depriving peaceful targets for government spending, such as hospitals and schools, as well as investment in industry.

The direct human cost

In the last ten years, in some 50 conflicts around the world, six million people have been killed, 90 percent of them civilians. Many millions more have been seriously injured, become homeless, or been forced to leave their homes and become refugees. Hundreds of thousands of children have become orphans as a direct result of war. Yet the struggle to survive is not over when a war ends. Thousands of people die from starvation or disease in war-torn countries unable to provide food, clean drinking water, and basic healthcare.

Do weapons make conflicts last longer?

In many cases, the availability of arms has prolonged conflicts and hindered attempts at building peace. Areas emerging from a war face major problems of crime, poverty, hunger, and disease. In addition, their industries, which provide jobs and income, as well as their basic infrastructure, such as road and rail systems, hospitals, and power supplies, are frequently devastated by the violence. While there may be a scarcity of many basic necessities, arms are often found in abundance. With policing systems frequently not present, criminals, armed groups, and even desperate civilians often seek to use arms to obtain food and water, to take control of a local area, or to seek revenge. Outbreaks of violence can lead to a conflict restarting.

A guerrilla fighter prepares to fire a grenade launcher in an already ruined city.

These refugees are fleeing from violence during the first Gulf War in 1991.

Do arms help to create refugees?

Refugees are civilian men, women, and children who have fled their homes in order to seek sanctuary in another country. Sometimes, refugees are created because of natural disasters such as earthquakes, volcanic eruptions, floods, or droughts. However, the most common cause of the many millions of refugees around the world is conflict involving arms. Bombardment from heavy weapons can destroy a town's houses, schools, factories, and hospitals, leaving nowhere to live or work. It can also destroy basic facilities such as clean water supplies. The use or threat of use of small arms can cause great fear and suffering. Fear of injury or death is a major reason why people leave their homes behind and take flight in order to seek safety elsewhere. Arms have enabled governments to force minority people out of their home territory or even the entire country. In the early 1970s, General Idi Amin banished the minority Asian peoples from Uganda, using arms directly or as a threat. Over 30,000 Ugandan Asians became refugees and had to leave the country and find homes elsewhere.

Despite the amount it costs to run the Mirage 2000 jet fighter, it still serves in the air forces of France, the United Arab Emirates, Egypt, Greece, India, Peru, Taiwan, and Qatar.

Do arms cause problems even if they are not used in war?

Many feel that the economic costs of buying large quantities of arms create as much hardship and misery as their actual use in battle. Governments have to make choices on what they spend their income. The more they spend on buying arms and building their military forces, the less money that remains to spend on essential, peacetime services such as health and education.

Arms are extremely expensive to buy. What is sometimes forgotten is that they also cost a huge amount to maintain, train personnel on, and use in peacetime. It costs around $2,700 to operate a Mirage 2000 jet fighter for just a single hour in peacetime. Many older aircraft have operating costs double that. In contrast, the average yearly income of a person in Africa is barely $600, less than two dollars a day. When

More spent on military than on health

In at least 84 countries, military spending exceeds spending on health. In more than one out of six developing countries, military spending actually exceeds the combined spending on all forms of health and education. There are 900 million people who cannot read and write in countries that spend more on arms and the military than they do on education.

Source: *The Human Development Report*, CAAT, 1997

hundreds of millions of the world's people face starvation and life-threatening diseases, critics of the arms trade argue that military spending is a luxury that cannot be afforded.

Why does arms spending particularly hurt less developed nations?

The world's less developed nations are mainly found in Asia, Africa, and South America. A large number of these are desperately poor and struggling, often unsuccessfully, to feed, clothe, and shelter their entire population. Yet many of these countries still spend large amounts of their budgets on buying arms, which they cannot build themselves. The value of all arms deliveries to developing nations in the year 2000 was $19.4 billion. This is a vast sum of money flowing out of poorer nations, usually into wealthier nations. Many critics of the arms trade argue that the majority of this money would be better spent inside a country's own borders in trying to solve basic problems of poverty and disease, or investing in its own industries rather than making other countries' industries rich.

Many African nations cannot afford to supply running water to a large proportion of their populations.

DEBATE—Does the arms trade restrict poorer countries' development?

- Yes. By offering loans and credit, the arms trade tempts nations to buy arms they cannot truly afford. The poorer nations that spend the most on arms often do not have a democratic system and free elections. Their governments stay in power using force.

- No. The arms trade simply offers products for sale. It is a government's choice to buy them or spend money on other things. If people do not like their government's decision, they can vote it out.

According to the organization Human Rights Watch, there are some 300,000 children fighting as soldiers in more than 30 countries.

DEBATE—Are child soldiers the arms trade's fault?

- Yes. The arms trade is partly to blame by building lethal and lightweight weapons easy enough for children to operate and by not stopping cheap weapons from reaching armed groups who use child soldiers.

- No. The arms trade cannot be blamed for a child's decision to fight in a war or the actions of people who force children to fight. Some children use arms simply to protect themselves and their families.

What problems do the world's children face with weapons?

The youngest people in society are often the most defenseless and without knowledge or understanding of the dangers or threats posed by weapons. According to UNICEF, the United Nations Children's Fund, over two million children are estimated to have died during armed conflicts in the last ten years. A further six million have been permanently disabled or seriously injured during the same period. Children, some of whom live in war zones and have grown up lacking education, cannot always read warning signs and tend to be curious by nature. As a tragic and common result, they often fall victim to landmines, unexploded bombs and shells, or wander unknowingly into the firing line.

Do children only suffer via weapons in war zones?

No. The wide availability of small arms in some countries has seen waves of violence with children as frequent targets. For example, in Colombia, some 4,000 children are killed with small arms every single year. The problem is also found in wealthier nations. Over 3,500 children and teenagers, for example, die every year in the US as a result of gun-related violence.

How many child soldiers are there?

The UN estimates that there are over 300,000 child soldiers currently fighting in conflicts around the world. Most are believed to be in their teens, but evidence has shown that many thousands are between eight and 12 years of age. Children are recruited into both official government military forces and into rebel groups. Many become soldiers because of poverty or a desire for revenge. Many more are forced to fight, as in Kendu's story at the start of this book. Military forces use children when a long war has seen the numbers of adults in an area fall dramatically. They are also used because they are easier to recruit and to bully into fighting with unquestioning obedience.

This child soldier is from the Southeast Asian country of Myanmar. According to Human Rights Watch, Myanmar has the largest number of child soldiers in the world.

What Is Being Done To Counter The Arms Trade?

Many people feel that the arms trade as it works today is wrong and produces undesirable, dangerous, and tragic effects. Work to counter the consequences of the arms trade occurs in many different ways: from the largest international conferences to the smallest mine clearing project.

A soldier sets fire to a pile of rifles collected during a gun amnesty in order to stop them from being used in future conflicts.

AROUND THE WORLD, many charitable groups and agencies are trying to reduce the impact of arms and conflict on parts of the world. Dozens of organizations lobby governments and the United Nations for changes to the ways weapons are bought, sold, and used around the world. Many other groups are concerned with the direct effects of arms use, treating war victims, rebuilding schools and hospitals, or helping refugees from conflicts settle in new places or return to their homes. Other organizations are seeking to remove arms in a region by reporting illegal arms trading where they find it taking place, through mine clearing operations, or through disarmament programs, such as arms amnesties. Arms amnesties are situations where illegally held weapons can be given up with no fear of being arrested, fined, or punished. In some cases, people are persuaded by being given money or another reward for each weapon that they surrender.

What are governments doing?

Many governments of wealthier nations, particularly those concerned about terrorists obtaining weapons, are investing huge sums of money into tracking and investigating illegal arms deals and trying to bring those who make them to justice. Large numbers of illegal sales are still being made around the world, but there have been some successes. In August 2003, Hemant Lakhani, an arms trader accused of trying to sell a missile to a terrorist group for use against an American passenger airliner, was captured. His arrest was the result of an 18-month operation involving intelligence agencies in the US, UK, and Russia. Many critics of governments' attempts to clear up the illegal arms trade maintain that these countries should be looking at the far bigger issue and creating much stricter laws on legal arms sales as well.

Disarming people in Albania

Vast amounts of arms are in circulation in Albania—as many as one for every four people. A UN project is successfully removing some of these weapons from circulation by striking deals with villages to surrender arms in exchange for community projects such as better electricity supplies or new roads. Seran Llaha, a member of Tudge, a village which has joined in the project, said; "I am very happy. All the village was involved. Giving in our guns is the first step for a safer, more peaceful future."

Source: Oxfam

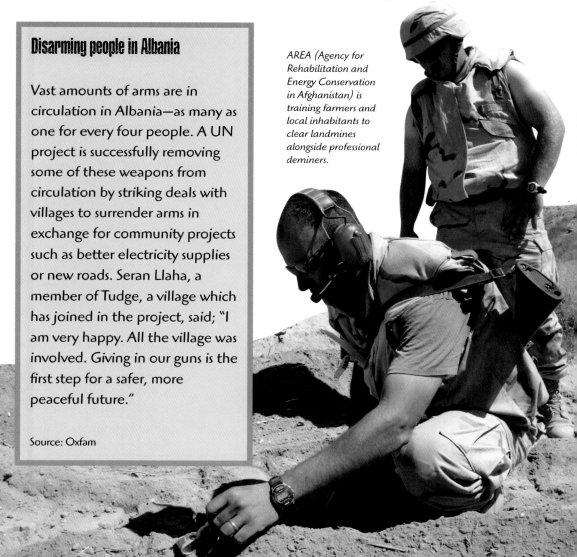

AREA (Agency for Rehabilitation and Energy Conservation in Afghanistan) is training farmers and local inhabitants to clear landmines alongside professional deminers.

What is an arms embargo?

Regulations on selling arms vary from country to country. Many nations have their own policies and refuse to sell certain types of arms or all arms to countries that are intent on war or use arms against their own people. Sometimes, countries group together, often using the United Nations, to impose an arms embargo—a ban on the sale of arms to a country. The UN arms embargo on South Africa, for example, started in 1977 and lasted until 1994. During that time, however, some arms supplies did manage to reach the country. Embargoes are rarely watertight as has been seen with arms reaching recently embargoed countries including Sierra Leone, Libya, and Iraq.

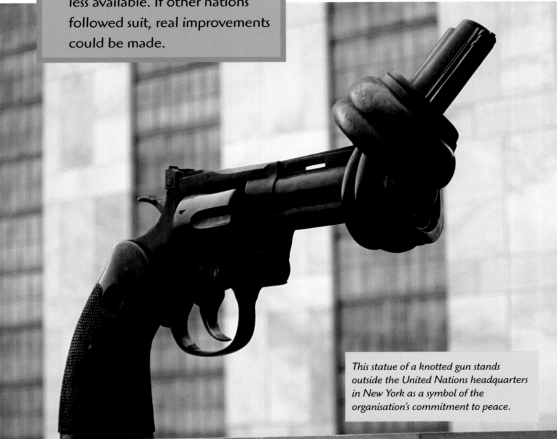

This statue of a knotted gun stands outside the United Nations headquarters in New York as a symbol of the organisation's commitment to peace.

A Hawk jet from the Indonesian Air Force, similar to those used by the Indonesian forces on their own people.

What is an end-use certificate?

In the UK, to get an export license, companies must now supply the government with an end-use certificate. This names who is buying the weapons and what they will use them for. While, in theory, this seems like a good idea, in practice, it does nothing to prevent an importer from promising to use arms for one purpose and then using them for another. For example, Hawk jet aircraft were sold by the UK to Indonesia with the intention of being used to patrol the country's borders. Instead, they were used in the summer of 2003 in attacks on Indonesia's own people in the Aceh province of the country.

License loopholes

Some arms companies have tried to bypass restrictions on arms sales by disguising the true contents of the trade. In 1996, an export license was granted to a British company called Procurement Services International Ltd. for six water cannons to Indonesia, a license that also included "associated equipment." UK parliamentary questioning eventually revealed that the "associated equipment" included over 300 armored personnel carriers made by the British company, Glover Webb. Despite this, the export license was not withdrawn by the UK government.

What international arms control agreements exist?

A number of international agreements on the sale and use of different weapons exist. These include the Biological Weapons Convention (1972) and the 1968 Nuclear Non-Proliferation Treaty (NPT). This latter agreement was designed to prevent nuclear weapons technology from being transferred all over the world. By early 2000, 187 countries had signed the NPT, including the five nations with known nuclear arms capability.

What was the Ottawa Treaty?

One of the most famous international arms agreements of recent years came into force in 1999. After years of campaigning, an agreement outlawing antipersonnel landmines was forged at the Ottawa Convention. The Ottawa Treaty bans the production, sale, and use of antipersonnel landmines and was signed by over 130 nations. It was hailed as a major breakthrough in controlling arms and has been backed by reports of at least 30 nations destroying their stockpiles of antipersonnel landmines.

US army soldiers check out antitank landmines planted by Iraqi forces in the Gulf War of 2003.

Diplomats applaud as the Ottawa Landmine Treaty is signed. The US refused to sign the treaty unless changes were made.

Do international agreements work?

International agreements have had some success. For example, with the breakup of the Soviet Union in the 1990s, many newly independent republics, such as Belarus, Ukraine, Georgia, and Kazakhstan, had Soviet nuclear weapons based on their soil, which they removed and decommissioned before signing the Nuclear Non-Proliferation Treaty.

However, for international agreements to work fully, all nations must sign and enforce the terms in the agreement. The three countries that are the largest producers of landmines—the United States, Russia, and China—have not signed the Ottawa Treaty. Nor have a number of other nations involved in current conflicts, such as Eritrea or Congo, or those in an arms race with rivals and neighbors, such as North and South Korea. In addition, some arms companies are working to find ways around the landmines treaty. They are developing or fitting antitank mines, which are not banned by the treaty, with highly sensitive trigger devices that can be set off by far less weight than a tank, such as a person or a small vehicle. While most nations around the world have signed the Nuclear Non-Proliferation Treaty, Israel, India, and Pakistan have not signed, and all three countries are believed to own or are in the process of developing nuclear weapons. In 2003, North Korea became the first nation to withdraw from the Nuclear Non-Proliferation Treaty and Iran decreased the level of access of international nuclear weapons inspectors to its nuclear facilities, leading to fears that both countries may be developing their own nuclear weapons.

Victims of landmines demonstrate outside the White House in Washington, D.C.

Can the public make a difference?

Faced with the huge size and power of the arms trade, backed by many national governments, it is tempting to believe that ordinary people are powerless. This need not be the case. By banding together in groups to protest and campaign against aspects of the arms trade, ordinary people can make a difference. For example, the Ottawa Treaty banning landmines was partly the result of prolonged campaigns in many countries by civilian groups. One organization, the International Campaign to Ban Landmines, received a Nobel Peace Prize in 1997 for its efforts in highlighting the damage landmines cause around the world.

Groups like the Campaign for Nuclear Disarmament (CND), Oxfam, Saferworld, and Campaign Against Arms Trade (CAAT) have highlighted and made public arms trade issues such as the government subsidies for weapons makers. Human rights groups like Amnesty International and Human Rights Watch publicize the atrocities committed by nations using arms. Topics like these were not discussed greatly in public in the past. Today, they are debated in the media, while pressure is put on governments to change laws and regulations.

Will the arms trade ever stop?

It is highly unlikely. Arms will always be developed, bought, and sold while nations exist and believe there are threats to their security. However, campaign groups believe it is possible to reduce the amount of arms bought and sold radically and increasingly restrict their use. Banning one type of weapon, reducing the sales of weapons to areas in conflict, or helping to disarm former fighters in a region may only seem like a small step. Yet it can make an enormous difference to the lives of many people.

Transform guns into hoes

Mozambique's civil war ended in 1992, but the large numbers of arms remaining in the country made rebuilding the nation extremely difficult. In 1995, the Mozambican Christian Council launched a campaign to "Transform Guns into Hoes." It sought to persuade people to hand over weapons in exchange for farming equipment, bicycles, and sewing machines. Thousands of guns, grenades, and landmines were traded in while people received useful, peaceful machines in return.

Children demonstrate against landmines outside 10 Downing Street, London, UK.

REFERENCE

Top 40 countries with the largest military budget in billions of dollars (2002)

US	399.1
Russia	65.0
China	47.0
Japan	42.6
UK	38.4
France	29.5
Germany	24.9
Saudi Arabia	21.3
Italy	19.4
India	15.6
South Korea	14.1
Brazil	10.5
Israel	9.4
Spain	8.4
Australia	7.6
Canada	7.6
Taiwan	7.0
Netherlands	6.6
Turkey	5.8
Singapore	4.8
Sweden	4.5
Iran	4.1
Kuwait	3.9
Norway	3.8
Greece	3.5
Poland	3.5
Argentina	3.3
UAE	3.1
Egypt	3.0
Belgium	2.7
Pakistan	2.6
Denmark	2.4
Vietnam	2.4
Colombia	1.7
Czech Republic	1.6
Iraq	1.4
North Korea	1.4
Philippines	1.4
Portugal	1.3
Libya	1.2

Sources: International Institute for Strategic Studies, US Department of Defense

Military spending as percentage of gross domestic product (top 15 and other selected countries)

1 Eritrea	29.4%
2 North Korea	25.0%
3 Angola	22.0%
4 Oman	13.0%
5 Saudi Arabia	13.0%
6 Nigeria	10.0%
7 Qatar	10.0%
8 Israel	9.4%
9 Kuwait	8.7%
10 Jordan	7.8%
11 Yemen	7.6%
12 Burundi	6.1%
13 Syria	5.9%
14 Turkey	5.6%
15 Malta	5.5%
US	3.2%
UK	2.7%
Spain	1.1%
Republic of Ireland	0.75%
Tanzania	0.2%

Source: Globastat

TOP 20 COUNTRIES BY NUMBERS OF ARMED FORCES PERSONNEL (2000)

1	China	2,810,000
2	Russia	1,520,000
3	US	1,366,000
4	India	1,303,000
5	South Korea	683,000
6	Pakistan	612,000
7	Turkey	610,000
8	Iran	513,000
9	Vietnam	484,000
10	Egypt	448,000
11	Ethiopia	352,000
12	Myanmar	344,000
13	Syria	316,000
14	Ukraine	304,000
15	Thailand	301,000
16	Indonesia	297,000
17	France	294,000
18	Brazil	288,000
19	Italy	251,000
20	Japan	237,000

Source: Nationmaster

LARGEST RECIPIENTS OF MAJOR CONVENTIONAL WEAPONS (1998–2002) IN MILLIONS OF DOLLARS

1	China	8,818
2	Taiwan	6,822
3	India	4,824
4	Turkey	4,688
5	Saudi Arabia	4,360
6	Greece	3,958
7	South Korea	3,445
8	Egypt	3,251
9	UK	3,116
10	Israel	3,033
11	Pakistan	2,992
12	Japan	2,799
13	UAE	2,092
14	Australia	2,044
15	Finland	1,898
16	Singapore	1,834
17	Algeria	1,784
18	Iran	1,440
19	Canada	1,309
20	Brazil	1,256
21	Malaysia	1,139
22	Netherlands	1,067
23	Switzerland	1,054
24	Angola	1,010
25	Spain	950
26	Italy	917
27	Norway	872
28	US	815
29	Argentina	790
30	Jordan	758

Source: SIPRI Database, 2003

Estimated cost of selected arms and military equipment (2002) in dollars

Aircraft and helicopters	Cost per unit	Manufacturer
B-2 Stealth bomber	$1 billion	Northrop Grumman
C-17 Globemaster transport	$232 million	Boeing
F-15 fighter	$105 million	Boeing
Eurofighter	$98 million	BAE Systems/EADS/Alenia Aerospazio
Global Hawk UAV	$75 million	Northrop Grumman
MH-47 Chinook helicopter	$67 million	Boeing
C130J Hercules transport	$55 million	Lockheed Martin
Pave Low helicopter	$40 million	Sikorsky
Tiger attack helicopter	$33.5 million	Eurocopter
Hawk trainer/fighter	$21 million	BAE Systems

Tanks, missiles and bombs		
Leopard 2 main battle tank	$10 million	Krauss-Maffei Wegmann
Tomahawk BlockIIIC cruise missile	$1.8 million	Raytheon
Storm Shadow cruise missile	$1.75 million	MBDA
AIM-120 AMRAAM missile	$386,000	Raytheon
Hellfire missile	$100,000	Boeing/Lockheed Martin
Stinger missile	$88,000	Hughes Missile Systems/Raytheon
AIM-9 Sidewinder missile	$41,300	Raytheon
Cluster Bomb—US CBU 87	$14,000	Alliant Techsystems

Small Arms		
M4 Automatic weapon & sight	$1,384	Colt
Uzi submachine gun	$1,100–1,700	Originally Israeli but many imitations
AK-47 Kalashnikov	$400–600	Originally Russian but many imitations

Source: Campaign Against Arms Trade (CAAT)

Leading suppliers of weapons (in millions of US dollars)

1	US	18,562
2	Russia	7,700
3	France	4,100
4	Spain	1,500
5	Germany	1,100
6	Israel	600
7	UK	600
8	China	400
9	Turkey	300
10	Sweden	200
10	Ukraine	200

Source: Conventional Arms Transfers to Developing Nations, 1993–2000

ESTIMATED LANDMINE NUMBERS IN SELECTED COUNTRIES (2001)

Afghanistan	4 million
Angola	200,000–6 million
Azerbaijan	50,000
Bosnia and Herzegovina	1 million
Cambodia	300,000–1 million
Chad	500,000
Colombia	70,000
Costa Rica	3,000–5,000
Croatia	1–1.2 million
Cyprus	17,000
Ecuador	50,000–60,000
Egypt	5–7.5 million
Eritrea	1.5–2 million
Ethiopia	1.5–2 million
Georgia	50,000
Guatemala	1,500–2,000
Honduras	15,000–35,000
Jordan	223,000
Lebanon	165,000
Morocco	1–2 million
Mozambique	800,000–1 million
Nicaragua	108,000
Rwanda	250,000
Sri Lanka	300,000
Syria	300,000
Thailand	1 million
Vietnam	3.5 million
Yemen	100,000
Zimbabwe	2.5 million

In addition, there are a number of countries including Israel, Iraq, Iran, Libya, Somalia, Sudan, and Zambia where the numbers of landmines are unknown but believed to be significant.

Source: *Hidden Killers 2001*, the US State Department

GLOSSARY

alliance Some form of partnership or agreement between two or more countries that are friendly to each other's interests.

amnesty A promise given by a government or police force not to punish someone for a crime.

arms race A situation where one or more nations buy arms and other nations feel threatened and respond by buying more arms themselves.

artillery Heavy guns that fire shells long distances.

binary chemical weapon A weapon containing two separate, relatively safe chemicals that when mixed form a dangerous and harmful substance.

biological weapons Use of living things or their parts or products to produce death, disease, or other harm in humans, animals, or plants.

boomerang effect The use of weapons against the interests of a country or organization that made and sold them in the first place.

boycott Cutting relations, such as trade, cultural, and government links, with a group or country.

brokering The buying, transport, and sale of arms in different countries.

chemical warfare The use of nonliving chemical substances, such as chlorine and phosgene and nerve agents including Sarin, to kill or harm people.

citizen A member of a country or other political community.

civilians People who are not in the armed forces.

civil war A war between opposing groups within one country.

Cold War Distrustful and hostile relationship between the Soviet Union and its allies and the United States and its allies that started shortly after World War II but never broke out into a full-scale world war. The Cold War ended in the early 1990s with the breakup of the Soviet Union.

convention A legal agreement to behave in a certain way made between two or more countries.

conventional weapons All weapons which are not biological, chemical, or nuclear. In practice, the term is usually used for larger weapons such as tanks, fighter and bomber aircraft, missiles, and artillery guns.

demining The removal of landmines from an area of land or water.

deployment The placement of weapons, forces, and equipment in a combat-ready position.

deterrent The holding of weapons by a country to deter an attack.

disarmament The reduction and dismantling or destruction of weapons.

dual-use products Equipment or products that can be used by both the military and civilians.

embargo An agreement made between some nations to stop the transfer of arms into or away from an area.

export license A certificate from a government granting permission to send equipment to another country.

Gross Domestic Product (GDP) A traditional measure of a country's economic strength and wealth. It represents the total value of all goods and services produced by a nation during a given year.

guerrillas Irregular soldiers who fight, usually by ambush and hit-and-run attacks.

human rights The basic rights of all people, such as the right to free speech, shelter, and food.

Intercontinental Ballistic Missiles (ICBMs) Missiles that can be fired from one continent and reach another thousands of miles away.

International Atomic Energy Agency (IAEA) A United Nations organization founded in 1957. Its goal is to promote the peaceful uses of nuclear technology, such as power production.

landmines A type of explosive weapon placed just underneath the land surface. They are triggered by pressure placed on the ground above them.

military coup When the armed forces of a country take over the running of the government, usually by force.

nonstate actor A term used to describe a rebel group within a country.

refugee A person taking refuge, especially in a foreign country, to escape troubles such as war, starvation, and political or religious persecution.

sanctions Penalties or punishments for breaking rules or agreements. Sanctions usually involve the withholding of trade from a country or region.

sanctuary A place of safety, free from harm or threat of harm.

small arms Types of handheld weapons, including pistols, rifles, and machine guns, that can be used by a single person.

state-actor Another term used to describe a country's government.

stockpile To build up large numbers of weapons or equipment.

subsidies Payments by governments or organizations to help fund the cost of a project or to reduce the running costs of a company.

superpower Term used to describe the United States and the Soviet Union during the Cold War era (1945–1991). Since 1991, the United States has been the world's only superpower.

surplus An amount of materials or equipment that has been left over after requirements are met.

terrorist group A group that uses violence or the threat of violence to try to achieve a goal.

treaty A strict agreement on a way of acting or not acting that has been made between nations.

Weapons of Mass Destruction (WMDs) A term used to describe nonconventional arms, including biological, chemical, and nuclear weapons.

FURTHER INFORMATION

BOOKS and MAGAZINES

The No-Nonsense Guide To The Arms Trade, Gideon Burrows, New Internationalist Publications Ltd. 2002
An up-to-date and comprehensive guide to the issues surrounding the arms trade around the world. The book contains personal examples of how the arms trade has affected individuals.

Just The Facts: The Arms Trade, Richard Bingley, Heinemann Library 2003
An explanation of where the arms trade is going which looks at arguments from both the defence manufacturers and antiarms-trade campaigners.

World Issues: The Arms Trade, Bernard Harbor and Chris Smith Rourke, Enterprises Inc. 1988
An easy-to-understand look at aspects of the arms trade and how and why it has grown in size and importance.

Small Arms Survey: Counting The Human Cost—Small Arms Survey, Oxford University Press 2003
The definitive guide to production and sale of small arms around the world with updated statistics on arms stockpiles and known illegal transfers.

The Arms Bazaar In The Nineties, Anthony Sampson, Coronet Books 1991
A fascinating history about the international arms trade detailing how arms buildups have occurred in many parts of the world.

The Arms Trade In The News, Adam Hibbert, Franklin Watts 2003
A collection of newspaper articles and explanations of different parts of the arms trade.

WEBSITES

http://www.acaat.org
Homepage of the Australian division of the Campaign Against Arms Trade.

http://defence-data.com
A website containing breaking news stories about the arms industry and trade deals.

http://www.landmineaction.org
The homepage of the campaign organization devoted to the elimination of landmines and assisting areas and individuals who have suffered because of landmines.

http://www.iaea.org
The website of the International Atomic Energy Agency which contains many reports and resources on nuclear weapons and how the IAEA and other organizations try to inspect sites and increase safety.

http://www.saferworld.org.uk
Homepage of an independent institute that researches ways to prevent armed conflicts around the world.

http://www.antenna.nl/enaat
Homepage of the European Network Against Arms Trade. This site contains up-to-date news, reports, and links to other arms trade resources.

http://www.cnduk.org
Website of the Campaign for Nuclear Disarmament, a group that campaigns for an end to nuclear weapons and other weapons of mass destruction.

ORGANIZATIONS

Campaign Against Arms Trade
11 Goodwin Street
London, UK
N4 3HQ
Tel: +44 20 7281 0297
Fax: +44 20 7281 4369
Website: http://www.caat.org.uk

**Coalition to Stop the Use of
Child Soldiers**
International Secretariat
2nd Floor
2–12 Pentonville Road
London, UK
N1 9HP
Tel: +44 20 7713 2761
Fax: +44 20 7713 2794
Website: http://www.child-soldiers.org
Email: info@child-soldiers.org

**Federation of American Scientists
Arms Sales Monitoring Project**
1717 K Street NW, Suite 209
Washington, D.C. 20036
Website: http://www.fas.org/asmp

**International Action Network on Small
Arms Transfers (IANSA)**
Box 422
37 Store Street
London, UK
WC1E 7BS
Tel: +44 207 523 2037
Website: http://www.iansa.org
Email: contact@iansa.org

Council For A Livable World
322 4th Street NE
Washington, D.C. 20002
Tel: 202 543 4100
Email: clw@clw.org

**International Campaign to Ban
Landmines**
110 Maryland Avenue NE
Box 6 , Suite 509
Washington, D.C. 20002
Tel: 202 547 2667
Fax: 202 547 2687
Email: icbl@icbl.org

Arms Control Association
1726 M Street NW, Suite 201
Washington, D.C. 20036
Tel: 202 463 8270
Fax 202 463 8273
Email: wade@armscontrol.org
Website: http://www.armscontrol.org

Arms Trade Resource Center
66 Fifth Avenue, 9th floor
New York
NY 10011
Tel: 212 229 5808
Fax: 212 229 5579
**Website:
http://worldpolicy.org/projects/arms**

INDEX

loans 33, 41
Lockheed 11, 54

machine guns 10, 18, 26, 57
metal detectors 23
Middle East 13, 29
mine clearing 44
  robots 23
minefields 22
Mirage 2000 fighter 40
Mirage Rafale fighter 16
missiles 16, 45, 54, 56, 57
mortars 8, 18
Mozambican Christian Council 51
Mozambique 51
muskets 10
mustard gas 20
Myanmar 43

Nagasaki 20
navigation systems 16
New York 46
nightsticks 16
Nobel Peace Prizes 50
nonstate actors 24, 25, 57
North Korea 21, 30, 49
Nuclear Non-Proliferation Treaty (NPT) 21, 48, 49
nuclear weapons 12, 16, 20, 21, 30, 48, 49, 56, 57

observers 29
oil 29
Ottawa Treaty 48, 49, 50
Oxfam 33, 45, 51

Pakistan 13, 21, 24, 28, 37, 49
Panama 27
Pentagon 13
Peru 40
phosgene gas 20, 56
police forces 17, 29
prestige purchasing 30, 31

prisons 17
Procurement Services International Ltd. 47

Qatar 40

radar 23, 34
rebels 8, 12, 19, 37, 57
refugees 38, 39, 44, 57
rifles 17, 18, 44, 57
riot shields 17
rocket launchers 8
Royal Air Force (RAF) 17
Russia 13, 15, 21, 45, 49

Saferworld 51
Saudi Arabia 15, 24
schools 37, 39, 44
security organizations 17
Sierra Leone 25, 46
Singapore 35
small arms 18, 19, 24, 43, 54, 57
soldiers 8, 19, 22, 29, 42, 43, 57
  child soldiers 42, 43
Somalia 27
South Africa 46
South America 12, 40
South Korea 24, 49
Soviet Union 12, 13, 19, 30, 31, 34, 37, 49, 56, 57
Sri Lanka 37
state actors 24, 25, 57
Stockholm International Peace Institute 14
Storm Shadow missiles 16, 54
strategic balance 35
submarines 16, 31
subsidies 33, 57
superpowers 12, 37, 57

Taiwan 24, 37, 40
Taliban 27
Tamil Tigers 37

tanks 11, 16, 49, 54, 56
tazer guns 17
tear gas 36
terrorists 21, 45, 57
Thailand 31
Tornado fighters 15
traders 10
Tudge 45
Tutu, Archbishop Desmond 43

Uganda 8, 9, 37, 39
UK 15, 21, 25, 26, 33, 45, 47, 48, 51
Ukraine 49
United Arab Emirates (UAE) 35, 40
United Nations (UN) 14, 15, 18, 19, 25, 29, 43, 44, 45, 46, 57
  Children's Fund (UNICEF) 42
  Peacekeepers 29
  Security Council 14, 15
US 9, 12, 13, 15, 19, 20, 21, 24, 27, 30, 31, 33, 34, 35, 37, 43, 45, 49, 56, 57

warships 10, 16
Washington, D.C. 13, 50
water cannons 17, 47
weapons inspectors 49
weapons of mass destruction (WMDs) 20, 21, 57
White House 50
World War I 10, 11, 20, 27
World War II 11, 12, 20, 34, 56

Zaharof, Sir Basil 10